A hundred years ago, central Africa was a land un-explored, shrouded in mystery, inspiring tales of strange peoples and vast unexploited wealth. This was the world that Cecil Rhodes, coming from the sheltered background of an English country vicar-age, was to enter and make his own. Tempted by tales of great fortunes to be made from the dia-mond mines at Kimberley, Cecil Rhodes set off in 1870 on a career that was to put his name, literally, on the world map

A cold, remote business genius, Rhodes devoted his entire energy to extending British influence in Africa. Under his instigation vast amounts of territory were annexed and mineral rights worth incalculable millions of pounds were aquired for a few rifles and trinkets. "I want to see all that red, British red; this is my dream," said Rhodes, and much of the dream became reality as thousands of pioneers trekked northwards from South Africa to run the new mines and settle the land.

The subject of this new *History Makers* title is a man who lived in an age when to be an Empire-builder was the height of patriotism, and who voiced the thoughts and ambitions of many British people; a man who left the world a legacy that perplexes us still – Rhodesia.

Cecil Rhodes

Neil Bates

WAYLAND PUBLISHERS LIMITED

WAYLAND HISTORY MAKERS

Frontispiece Cecil Rhodes (1853–1902)

SBN 85340 296 5
Copyright © 1976 by Wayland Publishers Ltd
First published in 1976 by
Wayland Publishers Ltd
49 Lansdowne Place, Hove, East Sussex BN3 1HS
Text set in 12/14 pt Photon Baskerville,
printed by photolithography, and bound in
Great Britain at The Pitman Press, Bath

Contents

List of Illustrations

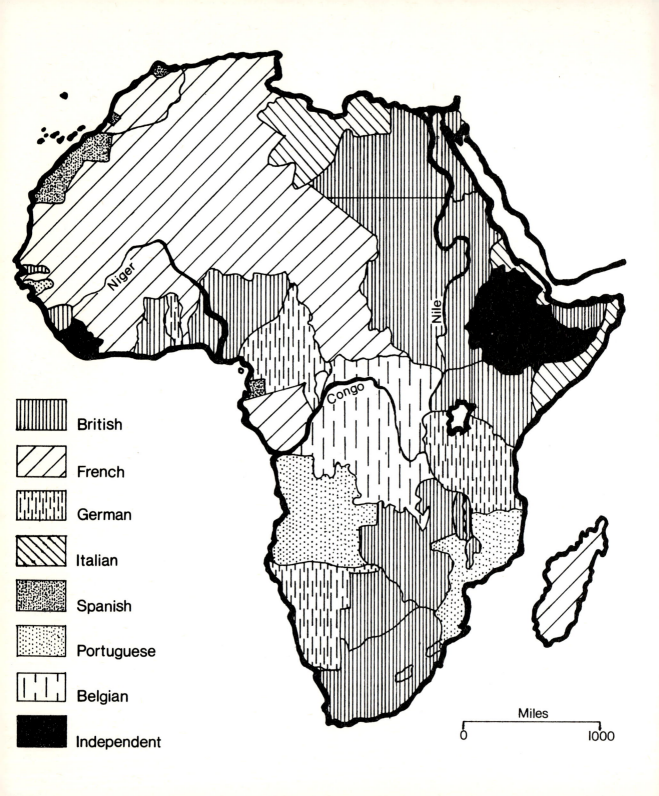

British

French

German

Italian

Spanish

Portuguese

Belgian

Independent

Niger

Congo

Nile

Miles

0   1000

Prologue

"What have you been doing since I last saw you, Mr Rhodes?" demanded Queen Victoria.

"I have added two Provinces to Your Majesty's dominions," Rhodes replied—December, 1894, an alleged conversation between Queen Victoria and Cecil Rhodes at Windsor Castle.

In the last half of the nineteenth century the British Empire was regarded by many people as a divinely-inspired system of government, of benefit to both the rulers and the ruled. At this time the Empire included India, Canada, Australia, New Zealand, South Africa and numerous other colonies, dependencies and territories scattered around the world. It was a fact of life—the foundation on which the wealth of Great Britain was built. Thousands left their homes to travel to the colonies, where the opportunities seemed limitless and fame and fortune lay just over the horizon. Nowhere was this more pronounced than in the pioneering society of South Africa.

In the last half of the seventeenth century the Dutch had established a settlement in South Africa, at the Cape of Good Hope. It was intended mainly as a supply base for Dutch ships trading with India and the east. Dutch colonists arrived to farm the land, and over the years they gradually moved into the sparsely-populated hinterland setting up farms and settlements. In 1795 the British occupied the Cape as a result of the Dutch alliance with France, which at that time was at war with Britain. The colony became permanently British in 1815.

To the Dutch settlers (or Boers as they were called from the Dutch word for farmer) British rule was distinctly unwelcome. The situation came to a head when, in 1833, Britain abolished slavery within the Empire. The Boers had long been slave-owners and were furious when their slaves were freed. Neither were they satisfied with the compensation paid to them by the British. The Boers simply wanted to run their own affairs without interference. So, rather than live under a government they disagreed with, many of them packed their wagons and trekked northwards, leaving the hated British behind. Beating back whatever native opposition they came across, they settled in the areas that were later to become the Transvaal, Natal and the Orange Free State.

Meanwhile Cape Colony, basically a farming community until diamonds were discovered in 1870, was gaining more independence in the conduct of its own affairs. The British Government, it was decided, would keep an eye on things but the colonists, including the Boers who had stayed behind, were to have a considerable amount of freedom in managing their own affairs under the Queen's representative, the British High Commissioner. Local councils were set up, and in 1852 the first Cape Parliament was formed on the lines of Westminster. Natal, which had been incorporated into Cape Colony in 1843, became a separate British colony in 1853, but it was not until 1857 that it set up its own parliament.

The British and the Boers of the Transvaal came to an agreement in 1852 which guaranteed the Dutch settlers the right to manage their own affairs without interference, on condition that they did not keep slaves or move south. The next year the British Government recognized the independence of the Boers in the Orange Free State.

There was continual friction between the Boers and the native tribes who lived on their borders, and because of this Basutoland, which bordered both the Orange Free State and Cape Colony, was brought under British protection. In 1871, it was incorporated into Cape Colony for a time. Bechuanaland to the north was also placed under British protection for the same reason.

Finally, in 1877, the British annexed the Transvaal because of further friction between the Boers and the native Africans. According to the British this move was made in order to avoid a native war, although such wars were a common occurrence at this time and the British themselves fought against the Zulus in 1879. The Transvaal Boers rose against the British in 1880 and several battles between British soldiers and Boer forces took place. But the British wanted to avoid a large-scale conflict and peace terms were agreed in 1881. The sovereignty of the Transvaal (which amounted to virtual independence) was recognized by the British and the situation developed into an uneasy calm until the Boer War finally erupted at the end of the century.

Such, then, was the troubled stage upon which Cecil Rhodes was to play his historic role.

Below A Boer home during the Transvaal Rebellion of 1880/1.

Cecil Rhodes as a young boy.

1. A Health Cure

Cecil Rhodes was a weak and sickly boy. He was born on 5th July, 1853. His family was a typical Victorian middle-class household, it was respectable, large (Cecil had six brothers and two sisters), and comfortably off. His father, Francis Rhodes, was the vicar of Bishop's Stortford in Hertfordshire. Cecil's parents were firm, but took an affectionate and lively interest in their children.

Because of his delicate health Cecil did not go to a private school like his brothers. He was sent instead to Bishop's Stortford Grammar School as a day-boy. He was never a brilliant pupil but was a hard and determined worker. History and geography were his best subjects. He liked games, especially cricket, and enjoyed long walks in the country. At the age of thirteen he made a vow never to marry as he felt it would interfere with the serious life that he wanted to lead. Unlike many other boys who have made similar resolutions Cecil never changed his mind! Although as a child he showed some of the qualities he was known for later in life, there was at this time no reason to think that he would amount to anything special.

He left the Grammar School when he was sixteen as Francis Rhodes wanted to conduct his son's education personally. The time had come to start thinking seriously about Cecil's future. The Reverend Rhodes wanted the boy to follow in his footsteps and enter the church.

> "My mother got through an amazing amount of work; she must have had the gift for organization, for she was never flustered, and seemed always to have ample time for all our many, and to us, important affairs. I think now we wore her out." *Cecil Rhodes.*

Cecil was more enthusiastic about law. Fate stepped in, however, when Cecil fell ill. The family doctor found that his lungs were very weak. As there was a family history of tuberculosis Cecil's parents decided that a sea voyage would do him good. His elder brother, Herbert, was at that time in South Africa in the colony of Natal where thousands of British pioneers were trying to make a living in a new land. Herbert was trying to grow cotton on the two hundred acres of land that he had bought. Now, it was decided, Cecil was to join him. Cecil was

Below Cecil Rhodes at about the time that he left Hertfordshire for South Africa in 1870.

thrilled at the idea. He was so excited that he found it impossible to sleep on the night before his voyage, so he got up and found a map of South Africa which he studied until dawn, "by which time Africa possessed my bones". On 21st June, 1870, he sailed on the ship *Eudora*. The boat docked at Durban, Natal, in September. Everything appeared "very rum" to the young Englishman. Herbert was not there to meet him. He had gone to look at the newly-discovered diamond mines at what was to become known as Kimberley.

Dr Sutherland, the Surveyor-General, invited Cecil to stay at his home until Herbert returned. Natal was a small colony that consisted mainly of a few miserable towns and farming settlements. There was a great deal of unrest and dissatisfaction amongst many of the people who lived there. Many were abandoning their farms and trekking to the diamond mines, lured by the chance of making a quick fortune. Cecil remarked in a letter home, "people here do nothing but talk about diamonds".

Below Durban looking "very rum" in about 1870, when Cecil Rhodes arrived there from England.

Like many other settlers Herbert Rhodes had not had a great success with his farm, but now that his brother was with him he was determined to do better. Cecil and Herbert lived in a small hut with only two beds and a table for furniture. Neither did they look very respectable. Cecil wrote to his mother, "I know you would be rather—well, what shall we say—disgusted—if you saw your two dear boys in shirt and trousers, with more holes than patches, all covered with brick dust . . .". But despite Herbert's determination their life in Natal did not improve. The price of cotton dropped from 10d. a pound to 6d. Grasshoppers and bollworms were ruining the crop, and the farm was plagued by baboons.

Below Life in a diamond miners' camp was very rough and hard.

With the lure of the diamond fields so strong, Herbert decided not to waste any more time on his farm working for no profit. He took a wagon and five natives and started for the mines. Cecil stayed behind to see that the cotton was picked, promising to join Herbert later. But he still felt that cotton was safer than diamonds, as can be seen from this letter: ". . . the cotton, the more you see of it, the more I am sure it is a reality. Not a fortune, and not attainable by everyone, but still, to one who has a good bit of land, money to start it properly . . . a very handsome income." The crop of cotton was very good but the price Cecil got for it was not. Disillusioned, he left for the mines and was never to return.

Below Oxen were nearly always used to make the long trail to the diamond mines.

The Kimberley Diamond Mine in the early 1880s, one of the most famous diamond mines in the world.
The finest diamond found in South Africa had come from this mine. It was named after its discoverer, a Mr Porter Rhodes, apparently no relation of the future Chairman of De Beers Consolidated Mines, Cecil Rhodes.

2. Diamonds

It was four hundred miles to the diamond fields. Herbert had taken eight of their oxen when he left and most of the remainder were unsuitable for Cecil to use on such a long journey. He thought of travelling light on horseback and doing the journey quickly. But, in the end, he decided that he would need an ox cart to carry his provisions, although he did ride on horseback himself. He took with him such things as biscuits, flour, tea, sugar, a bucket and spade, books, and for his weak chest—"that wonderful box of lozenges my father sent me."

The trip took a month. Cecil always had to be on his guard because of the risk of being attacked by marauding bandits. As it was, some of his bags "disappeared", including a treasured copy of Plutarch's *Lives*. When at last he reached his destination, Herbert, for some reason best known to himself, left Cecil to look after his diamond claims and set off back to the farm to look at the cotton. Cecil settled down to the hard life of a miner. The claims were at Colesburg Kopje, soon to be known as Kimberley, in Cape Colony. (The diamonds had been discovered there in 1870.) Within a year no less than ten thousand people were working there, digging, panning, sweating and cursing. "Men from every corner of the world plus," as Rhodes put it, "natives who have come to work for diamonds, to steal diamonds and to lay their earnings out in rifles and powder." It was a rough, and dangerous place. Some historians have said that the Wild West of America was tame compared to the

> "What above all else had counted was that Africa was a political vacuum into which the boundless greed of Europe was bound to penetrate." *Colin Cross: The Fall of the British Empire.*

> "Fancy an immense plain with right in its centre a mass of white tents and iron stores, and on one side of it, all mixed up with the camp, mounds of lime like anthills; the country is all flat with just thorn trees here and there." *Cecil Rhodes describing the diamond fields in a letter home, 1871.*

19

Kimberley diamond mines! Shootings were an everyday occurrence. Prostitutes were in abundance, and they had no shortage of clients! There was one bar for every sixteen inhabitants. Not surprisingly many of the miners died of drink without any sign of the fortunes they had come to make. Fresh water cost a shilling a bucket and fresh vegetables ten shillings each.

Surprisingly, Rhodes fitted easily into this society of riff-raff and fortune hunters, although some descriptions of him at this time are not what you would expect of a miner in South Africa. "A tall fair boy, blue eyed, and with somewhat aquiline features, wearing flannels of the school playing fields somewhat shrunken with strenuous rather than effectual washings", was how a fellow miner described him. To others he appeared as a "compound of moody silence and impulsive action . . . hot and violent at times". It was at this time that Cecil met a young man who was to become not only a business partner, but also one of his closest friends, Charles Rudd, who had also come out from Britain. Rudd had only one fault as a partner. He could not keep up with the tremendous amount of drinking which formed such a large part of life at Kimberley.

Opposite Page There was a great shortage of female dancing partners in the mining towns of South Africa—the miners had to make do with each other. The picture shows a "bull dance" in full swing, in a canteen in the Transvaal in 1887.

Below Hard drinking was also part and parcel of the South African mining scene in the late nineteenth Century—but the miners still needed a good night's sleep . . .

21

In 1872 Cecil Rhodes had a mild heart attack, the result of working too hard at the mines. Herbert, who had recently returned to Kimberley, suggested that a trip to the north would help his brother's recovery. They had heard a rumour that gold had been discovered in the Transvaal and had high hopes of finding some. Cecil eventually recovered from the attack, but the brothers were bitterly disappointed to find that the tales of gold had been exaggerated. They decided to return to Kimberley. But when they arrived back at the diamond fields Herbert Rhodes decided to move on yet again. Cecil Rhodes and Charles Rudd bought up his claims. They never saw Herbert again. After a series of adventures he died in 1879, when a keg of rum burst and caught fire in his tent in Nyasaland. He was burned to death.

Soon the Rhodes/Rudd partnership was making a name for itself. Together Rhodes and Rudd worked with pick and shovel to make a success of the claims. They were lucky. The land proved to be rich diamond-bearing ground, and, with the primitive equipment the partners possessed and with the help of native workers, they began to make good. In a letter to his mother Cecil wrote, "I average about £100 a week." In those days this was no mean sum.

Left A licensed diamond buyer's office
in Kimberley in the 1870s.

3. "Make your country a source of light . . ."

Below **Rhodes at Oxford with two friends: R. Dundas Graham (Bottom) and Norman Garstin (top).**

Although he was successful at Kimberley, Rhodes' heart had long been set on going to Oxford University. He had always been unhappy with the education he had received at Bishop's Stortford. Now, finding himself with enough money to fulfil his ambition, he booked passage on a ship for England, leaving Charles Rudd in charge of the claims. He was so ill equipped for this return to England that during the trip his one and only pair of trousers "started to fall to pieces and had to be repaired with sail cloth".

Rhodes was accepted as an undergraduate by Oriel College, and in October 1873, started his first term. Oxford was all he had hoped it would be. It offered him the chance of serious reading, lectures and long discussions, together with sports such as rowing and polo. These years at Oxford had a tremendous effect on him. He arrived there without any clear idea of what to do with his life. When he left he had developed into the man who was to change the face of Africa. He was older than most of the undergraduates but was soon accepted by them as "a character"—someone who had seen a world very different to the one they were used to. As a student he got into several scrapes, and once was nearly caught going to the forbidden horse races at Epsom—"but still do not think I shall be sent down".

At Kimberley Rhodes had been happy simply making money. Now, living at Oxford and travelling to Africa at intervals, he began to realize that to make money was not a sufficient purpose in life. A lecture given at Oxford by John Ruskin, the writer and philosopher, captured Rhodes' imagination and helped direct him along the path he was to follow for the rest of his life. "Have a fixed purpose of some kind for your country and yourselves," Ruskin had said, ". . . make your country for all the world a source of light, a centre of peace . . . this is what England must do or perish: she must form colonies abroad as far and as fast as she is able."

Encouraged by sentiments such as these, Rhodes came to believe that the British had been chosen by God to create a world-wide society based on liberty, peace and justice. This was an opinion that many people in Victorian England would have agreed with. The effect upon Rhodes of these trends of thought and of writers like Ruskin is seen in the amazing will that he made at Oxford. In the event of his death, all his money and possessions were to go to the Government so that a secret organization could be formed to work for "the extension of British rule throughout the world" and "the ultimate recovery of the United States of America as an integral part of the British Empire".

Although he later modified these ideas he never completely abandoned them. They were to mark his entire life. But now Rhodes felt that he had to achieve something himself, and he turned his attention on Africa. During his visits to Kimberley, Rhodes had urged Charles Rudd to "accumulate the ready". By increasing their few thousand pounds Rhodes planned to finance his scheme to extend the British Empire in Africa. He had a purpose in life now, but a great deal of money was needed to make it a reality.

Above John Ruskin (1819–1900), the English author, art critic and philosopher who roused England to a sense of responsibility for the squalor in which commercial competition had involved the country, and who so inspired Cecil Rhodes at Oxford.

"I contend that we are the first race in the world, and that the more of the world we inhabit, the better it is for the human race . . . Added to which the absorption of the greater portion of the world under our rule simply means the end of all wars." *Cecil Rhodes.*

4. Return to Africa

In 1878 Rhodes left Oxford and returned to Kimberley. The town was no longer as wild as it had been in its heyday. Diamond stealing and illicit diamond buying (IDB) which had always been great problems, were not now so widespread, and the bad characters who had made the town so dangerous and exciting had moved on to new frontiers. Hotels and shops had been opened and many miners had encouraged their families to come out and join them. There was no railway as yet—everything still had to be brought in by teams of oxen. Water above ground was so scarce that men were known to take baths with bottled soda water. But unfortunately in the mines themselves there was too much water.

On his return, Rhodes found that the yellow ground in which diamonds had originally been found had been exhausted. Underneath was blue clay. Many people were sure that no diamonds would ever be found in it and decided to sell out. Rhodes and Charles Rudd bought up as many of these claims as they could. Although they were not experts in geology, they were sure that diamonds would continue to be found. They were right!

The partners were determined eventually to control all the diamond production in Kimberley. They formed a limited company to enable them to take advantage of any opportunities that came up. This meant that they would be able to raise money to finance their business more easily than before.

They did not limit themselves to mining. They pur-

"Already . . . Rhodes was thinking in terms not of a controlling interest in the de Beers mine only but of a controlling interest in the whole field, which would enable the output, and therefore the price, of diamonds to be controlled." *John Marlowe: Rhodes.*

Above An awe-inspiring view of the great diamond mine at Kimberley, sketched in 1881.

sued any project that might make them money. On one occasion they gained a contract to pump a mine clear of water. Only one thing was lacking—the pump itself. One had to be found fast. But the rains arrived, and it was impossible to travel the three hundred miles to the nearest railway to collect it. The partners somehow had to persuade the understandably annoyed mine-owners to give them more time. Rhodes went to see them, and unbelievably succeeded. Henry Hawkins, a fellow miner said, "I have never forgotten the way in which he, still quite a youth, handled that body of angry men . . ." Eventually they succeeded in getting a pump and clearing the mine.

Right Barney Barnato (1852–1897), the English financier who backed Cecil Rhodes and made a huge fortune from diamonds in South Africa.

Below Alfred Beit (1853–1906), British financier and a close friend of Cecil Rhodes. *Below right* Dr Leander S. Jameson (1853–1917), close colleague of Rhodes.

At this point Rhodes met three men who were to have a great effect on his life. Barney Barnato, originally from Whitechapel in London, had arrived in South Africa as Rhodes was on his way to Oxford. For Barnato, anything which promised a quick financial return was worth trying. He was the sort of man destined to succeed in the South Africa of the time. Sharp, crafty and always on the lookout for a nice profit, he was also patriotic, generous and had a good sense of humour. At the fields he had gone from strength to strength, and with hard work and luck he became one of the foremost figures in Kimberley.

The second man, Alfred Beit, was the son of a German businessman who knew almost everything there was to know about diamonds. "When I reached Kimberley," he had said, "I found very few people knew anything about diamonds; they bought and sold vaguely and a great many of them really believed that the Cape diamonds were of a very inferior quality. Of course I saw at once that some of the Cape stones were as good as any in the world." Alfred Beit and Cecil Rhodes became very close friends. Each trusted the other completely. Without Beit it is doubtful that Rhodes would have achieved as much as he did. Sir Percy FitzPatrick, a friend of both said, "There can be no doubt whatever that Beit was Rhodes' financial genius."

Dr Leander S. Jameson also became a close colleague. Driving on his rounds in a smart carriage he became one of the familiar sights of the town. Gay, witty and addicted to gambling, he would have been a well-known character wherever he went. In one poker game he staked everything, horse, carriage and household effects, lost them all and won them back the same night. Jameson was later to be involved in a fiasco which nearly ruined both Rhodes and himself.

Above **Barney Barnato—by the famous cartoonist "Spy".**

"Jameson was as odd a doctor as ever took the oath. The son of a Scottish lawyer . . . he would seem on paper cut out for a life of cautious convention—a sound Edinburgh family physician, perhaps, or the trusted confidant of lairds. Instead his life was one of rip-roaring excitement." *James Morris: Pax Britannica.*

5. A Public Figure

Below Mealtime in a Boer household in 1881.

Rhodes' interest in the wider political scene was growing. His grand plan for a British Empire in Africa was becoming more than a youthful dream, but to have any chance of success he believed he must hold political power. On looking at a map of Africa he once said "I want to see all that red, British red; this is my dream". To further that ambition he stood for the seat of Barkly West, in Cape Colony.

Most of the electors in Barkly were Boer farmers. Rhodes recognized that "the Dutch are the coming race in South Africa, and they must have their share in running the country". He won the seat and held it until his death. Only a man of his exceptional qualities could have held the loyalty of the Boer farmers when they were quite ready to take up arms against Britain herself. In March 1881 he entered the Cape Parliament for the first time.

He soon settled into his new surroundings, and certainly made an impression on his fellow politicians. "Watch that man," said one well-known political figure, "he is the future man of South Africa and possibly of the world." Another was heard to complain, "He is never still from the time he enters the house until he leaves it."

Of the problems facing the Cape Government at this time, that of Basutoland was one of the most urgent. The Prime Minister of the Cape, Gordon Sprigg, wanted to disarm the Basuto tribe and rule them directly from Cape Town. Their chief, Letsie, had little faith in the Government's ability to look after its subjects, and believed that the Basutos would be safer if they kept their weapons and enjoyed some freedom to decide things for themselves.

Above **Basuto tribesmen.**

Rhodes' first speech was on the Basuto problem. He knew the Basutos well for many worked in the mines. He also thought it unjust that they should be forced to give up their guns after working hard in bad conditions for the money to buy them. Furthermore, Rhodes realized that if the Basutos were disarmed they might refuse to work for the mining companies and there would be a grave shortage of labour.

Rhodes was not a good public speaker. His grammar was poor and he had a squeaky voice, but he made it quite clear that he did not like the accepted way of doing things in Parliament. His sincerity and wide-ranging mind held people's attention. When he spoke everybody listened. Sprigg was defeated and forced to resign. The Basutos were allowed to keep their guns.

"Side by side with the tendency to decentralization in local affairs, there is growing up a feeling for the necessity of greater union in Imperial matters. The primary tie which binds our Empire together is one of self-defence. The Colonies are already beginning to cooperate with and contribute to the mother country for this purpose, but if they are to contribute permanently and beneficially they will have to be represented in the Imperial Parliament where the disposition of their contributions must be decided on . . ."
Cecil Rhodes

Above Jan Hofmeyr (1845–1909), leader of the powerful Boer farmers organization, the Afrikaaner Bond.

"He . . . had an amusing and characteristic encounter with a child. 'My boy,' he said expansively, 'I'll send you to Oxford.' 'No, you won't,' retorted the boy, and Rhodes, who liked the young to stand up to him, was delighted." *Lockhart and Woodhouse: Rhodes.*

"Widely different in character though they were, they soon found common ground, not least perhaps in the fondness of both men for an unconventional approach to any task they were attempting." *Lockhart and Woodhouse on the meeting between Rhodes and General Gordon in their book, Rhodes.*

In Parliament, Rhodes came to know Jan Hofmeyr, the leader of the "Afrikaaner Bond", an organization of Boer farmers which held a great deal of political power. If the Bond was against it no government could survive. When the two first met neither was particularly impressed. Hofmeyr had been told that Rhodes was a "regular, beefsteak Englishman", and Rhodes thought of Hofmeyr as a dangerous, subversive character. After being introduced however, they came to realise that their aims for the future of South Africa were very similar.

Although Sprigg had resigned, the trouble with the Basutos continued. The Government received an offer from the famous British soldier, General Gordon, then, in his own words, "supervising the barracks and drains of Mauritius", to try and solve the problem. General Gordon reached Cape Town in May 1882, and decided to call a series of tribal meetings in Basutoland. Rhodes was asked to go with him. He was extremely impressed by Gordon who appeared unarmed at these gatherings, and followed his example. General Gordon liked Rhodes' forcible character and came to the conclusion that together they would make a strong team. "Stay with me and we will work together," he said to Rhodes. But Rhodes turned him down. "There are very few men in the world to whom I would make such an offer," Gordon replied, "but of course you will have your way. I never met a man so strong for his opinion; you think your views are always right."

Gordon resigned after an argument with the Government. He never saw Rhodes again, and two years later was killed by the Dervishes at Khartoum in the Sudan. Rhodes was deeply shocked when he heard of his death. "I am sorry I was not with him", he often said. The Basuto problem was later settled when, in 1883, Basutoland became a British protectorate, administered by a resident British official.

General Charles Gordon (1833–85).

6. Expansion of Interests

Above **Johannes Nicholas De Beer,** the original owner of the farm on which the De Beers Mine was discovered.

"Barney Barnato, . . . confessed . . . that 'when you have been with him half an hour you not only agree with him, but come to believe you have always held his opinion . . . Rhodes has an extraordinary ascendancy over men . . . You can't resist him: you must be with him.'" *A. J. Hanna: The Story of the Rhodesias and Nyasaland.*

Although he was involved in politics Rhodes had not forgotten his business interests. The De Beers Company which he had started with Charles Rudd had bought up many claims. It was named after the Boer farmer who originally owned the land Kimberley grew up on. If he was to gain control of the whole diamond field Rhodes still had to deal with certain rivals the most important of whom was Barney Barnato. Rhodes tried to persuade Barnato to join him and form a large company to control the mines. Barnato was not enthusiastic, as he would have preferred to remain in charge of his own company and make decisions for himself.

Rhodes decided that the only way of getting what he wanted was to buy enough shares in Barnato's mining company to gain control. Because he wanted the shares so badly he was willing to pay far more than they were worth. As a result the price of the shares rose fantastically. Even friends and colleagues of Barnato could not resist the temptation of making such profits and sold their shares. Rhodes, with the backing of Alfred Beit, bought up the shares as soon as they came on the market. In the end Rhodes held three-fifths of the shares and Barnato was forced to come to an agreement. With the power of his new large business behind him, Rhodes managed to buy out the other smaller companies. He had now got what he wanted—control of all the diamond mines currently in operation, and as new mines were started they were taken over by the De Beers Company which at one time controlled 90% of the world's diamond production.

Then came news of a really big gold strike. It was no rumour, as similar news had previously been. Extremely rich deposits of gold had been found on the Witwatersrand, high ground south of Pretoria. Although Rhodes was not as quick off the mark as some, as soon as he was convinced of the quality of the newly discovered gold he moved in and bought nine claims on the Rand. Rhodes was never as interested in gold as he was in diamonds, but Consolidated Gold Fields of South Africa Ltd., the company he set up to exploit and run his gold interests, was his most successful business. The gold

"[Rhodes] had a Roman face, big, prominent of eye, rather sneering—just such a face as a police reconstruction might compose, if fed the details of one who was both a diamond millionaire and a kind of emperor." *James Morris: Pax Britannica.*

Below A cartoon from the *Westminster Gazette* showing Rhodes as a "Kimberley Frog" trying to make himself bigger than "the Bull" (i.e. England).

President Paul Kruger (1825–1904) at his home in about 1900.

had been discovered in the Boer republic of the Transvaal. The town of Johannesburg later grew up on the site. Paul Kruger, the President of the Transvaal, had no objection to miners coming in to dig for gold, so long as they paid taxes to his Government. But he did not want them to have any say in how the country was run, and this was to cause a great deal of trouble later on.

Pleased with his success in the diamond and gold fields, Rhodes turned his attention once more to his grand plan for Africa. To the north, in Central Africa, lay Matabeleland, a region with a moderate climate suitable for Europeans. Rhodes was determined that this should become part of the British Empire. However, Kruger was also interested in the area. He thought it an ideal place for Boer farmers to move into.

In 1884 Germany claimed land on the east coast as colonies. The Cape Government realized that if Germany was to be stopped from moving into Matabeleland,

"That young man will cause me trouble if he does not leave politics alone and turn to something else." *President Kruger, speaking of Rhodes*

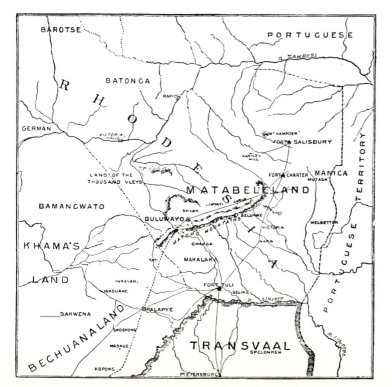

Left Map of Matabeleland.

37

the British would have to take control of Bechuanaland, which lay on the north west border of Cape Colony. Then the way northwards would be left free. On Rhodes' advice British troops under the command of Sir Charles Warren were sent into Bechuanaland where Rhodes joined them—"wearing a big slouch hat, and a very dirty pair of white flannel trousers with old tennis shoes as his footgear." Sir Charles was not impressed! A meeting was arranged with Kruger to try and reach a solution acceptable to both the Transvaal and Cape Colony. Although this was the first meeting between Rhodes and Kruger, the President of the Transvaal was heard to say afterwards, "that young man will cause me trouble." Kruger was not pleased by what was decided. Military law was declared throughout Bechuanaland and Sir Charles Warren ordered that the country was to be settled only by those of British origin.

The way was now open for expansion into the interior. Rhodes' plans for Africa were almost within reach.

"Money is power, and what can one accomplish without power?" *Cecil Rhodes*

7. Lobengula and the Concession

The Matabele, a warrior tribe, were among the fiercest fighters in Africa. They had been driven northwards by Boer settlers earlier in the century. Now their nation lay in the path of the British. Lobengula, their king, was an intelligent man, with more awareness of the outside world than might be expected. He was confident that he could cope with a few wandering white men, for hunters and adventurers were often to be found in his domain. But he knew his impis, or regiments, could not stand against a large white army. His 15,000 warriors were never happier than when they were terrorizing weaker tribes, burning villages and carrying off children to be brought up as slaves. Lobengula himself wanted nothing more than to be left alone with his wives—he had more than sixty. He had no interest in gold or diamonds.

Although he was in many ways a traditional native chief, Lobengula was no dictator. He always considered the advice of his wise men before coming to a decision. However, he was capable of extremely cruel behaviour. One account tells of a man who was unwise enough to be caught stealing the royal beer. Lobengula first had his lips cut off, as they had tasted the beer. Then he ordered the unfortunate man's nose which had smelt the beer, to be sliced off, and his forehead peeled down to cover his eyes, which had seen the beer. As if this was not enough the thief was taken away and fed to the crocodiles!

Below The Matabele king, Lobengula (*c.* 1832–1894).

There are many eye-witness accounts of this somewhat fearsome figure, but Sir Sidney Shippard, who was Her Majesty's Commissioner in Bechuanaland, gives us a picture that is probably the most realistic. "In person he is rather tall and very stout, though by no means unwieldy. . . . His colour is a fine bronze and he evidently takes great care of his person and is scrupulously clean. He wears the leathern ring over his forehead as a matter of course. . . . Like all the Matabele warriors, who despise a stooping gait in a man, Lobengula walks quite erect, with his head thrown back and his broad chest expanded and as he marches along at a slow pace with his long staff in his right hand, while all the men round shout his praises, he looks the part to perfection." His usual clothing was a kilt of monkey skins.

Lobengula's main kraal, or town, was at Bulawayo —"the place of slaughter". He had two brick houses that had been built for him by a sailor, but preferred living in an old ox-wagon. He was probably one of the best kings that the Matabele had ever had, but even he could not hold out against the European civilzation in the south.

Lobengula's part in European colonial history began shortly before in December, 1887, when Rhodes heard a rumour that if true could ruin his plans. Kruger had apparently signed a treaty with the Matabele king. He had sent a man called Pieter Grobler to Bulawayo, and Lobengula had signed a document putting his country under the protection of the Transvaal. On the face of it this did not mean much, but the Boers thought it gave them the right to move into Matabeleland. Lobengula later denied that he had signed anything. It is certainly true that no-one had heard of the place where the treaty was supposed to have been signed, and the witnesses could never be traced. Rhodes decided to act, and with the agreement of Sir Hercules Robinson, the British High Commissioner, he sent a letter to John Moffat, the

Opposite Page King Lobengula in his favourite seat.

"Lobengula wanted to trust the Europeans, and wanted them to trust him. He was, and proved himself within wide limits, a man of honour." *A. J. Wills: The History of Central Africa.*

son of a missionary, who was travelling in Matabeleland. He asked Moffat to find out if the rumour was true, and also to get Lobengula to sign a treaty with the British.

When Moffat approached the king at Bulawayo, Lobengula said, "I want no Boers. They stole my father's country and would like to come here and steal mine." He seemed to think the British were different, and after very little persuasion signed a treaty with Moffat. When news of Moffat's success reached Cape Town, Rhodes decided to send three messengers to Lobengula. He was afraid that other people might try to take advantage of the situation first. Although officially he wanted the king to grant him mineral rights, his real interest was neither gold nor diamonds: "If we get the whole of Matabeleland, we shall get the balance of Africa," he was heard to remark.

His messengers, Charles Rudd, F. R. Thompson, and Rochfort McGuire, reached Bulawayo in September, 1888. They presented Lobengula with one hundred gold sovereigns, a gift from Rhodes, and thought the king "a very fine man." Whilst discussions were going on they were fed "like lions at the zoo", with "masses of partly cooked meat on sticks", and were expected to drink "vast quantities of tepid beer." They enjoyed their stay, and by the end of October Lobengula had signed an agreement. The king was to receive £100 every month plus one thousand rifles with ammunition. A steamboat "with guns suitable for defensive purposes" was also included but apparently was never delivered. In return Cecil Rhodes was granted "the complete and exclusive charge over all metals and minerals situated and contained in [Lobengula's] kingdom . . . together with full powers to do all things they deem necessary to win and procure the same." The extent of these rights was considerable, and Lobengula could not have realized exactly what he had let himself in for. He thought that no more than ten white men would come into Matabele-

"He received his visitors in his cattle-kraal, a stinking, shadeless place which swarmed with flies; to impress them with his importance he kept them waiting there for some time before deigning to appear." *A. J. Hanna: The Story of the Rhodesias and Nyasaland.*

"All the panoply of a modern state was extracted from the concession of mineral rights which was all that Lobengula thought he had given away." *Lockhart and Woodhouse: Rhodes.*

land to dig for gold and diamonds. Later, when he realized the truth, he said he had been tricked into signing the agreement.

Rhodes himself was very pleased. The concession was just what he wanted. Other people were not so happy. They were worried about giving the Matabele so many weapons, but calmed down when it was pointed out that the Matabele were such bad marksmen that they were not likely to do much damage with the rifles anyway.

Above Matabele warriors setting off for battle.

" . . . it must be admitted that the treatment of Lobengula does not form a chapter in the history of Africa of which white men should be proud."
Lockhart and Woodhouse: Rhodes.

43

Cecil Rhodes addressing the
shareholders of the British South
Africa Company.

44

8. London and the Charter

In March, 1889, Cecil Rhodes arrived in London. He had decided that a Charter Company was needed to get the most out of Lobengula's concession. This meant no other company could move into the area; he would have a monopoly. In return for granting the charter the British Government would exercise some control over the company's actions. Diplomatic assistance would be available to the company if required. The company would take most of the trouble and expense of empire-building out of the Government's hands. Rhodes found that many people were opposed to his activities. By now they realized that he could never be content with a simple business operation. He had made his views too well known. The Aborigine's Protection Society which looked after the interests of natives in various parts of the world, was concerned that if Rhodes were granted the powers he wanted, Africans would be badly treated. The London Chamber of Commerce was also against him but for slightly more mercenary reasons. They believed that other companies should be allowed to take advantage of the concession.

To win support, Rhodes needed the help of people with political influence. He already had the backing of Lord Rothschild, the banker. Rothschild was a friend of Alfred Beit. He had supplied some of the money that had enabled Rhodes and his friends to amalgamate the

> "You have many instincts. Religion, love, money-making, ambition, art and creation, which I think from a human point of view the best, but if you differ from me, think it over and work with all your soul for that instinct you deem the best." *Cecil Rhodes*

Above left Sir Hercules Robinson (1824–1897), the Governor of the Cape and High Commissioner for South Africa (1880–1889), and Governor and Commander in Chief of Cape Colony (1895–1897)—at the time of the Jameson Raid. *Above right* Lord Knutsford (1825–1914), Colonial Secretary (1887–1892). *Left* Charles Stewart Parnell, (1846–1891) leader of the Irish Nationalists Home Rule Party, to whom Rhodes had given £10,000.

diamond mines, and had great confidence in their experience and ability.

Rhodes also received help from Sir Hercules Robinson who knew many influential people and set himself the task of persuading them that Rhodes was right. Lord Salisbury, the Prime Minister, agreed with the main outline of Rhodes' plan. He too wanted to see all South and Central Africa under the British flag, but he drew the line at Rhodes' plan for a railway running from the Cape to Cairo through British territory. The Prime Minister said, "I cannot imagine a more inconvenient possession," although he was perfectly agreeable to a chartered company financing his own imperial visions.

Lord Knutsford, the Colonial Secretary, was also interested in Rhodes' ideas for extending British influence, although to begin with he did not take a particularly good view of Rhodes. This was because sometime before Rhodes had given £10,000 to Charles Parnell, the leader of the Irish Nationalist Party, the party that was committed to Home Rule for Ireland. Rhodes, however, had attached a condition to this gift to which Parnell had agreed. He had insisted on the continuation of Irish representation in the British Parliament if any sort of independence should be granted. Rhodes believed that this would enable other self-governing colonies to send members to Parliament, giving birth to "a closer union of the Empire." When the two men finally met, Knutsford was impressed by Rhodes, and recommended that the charter should be granted. "Such a body may to some considerable extent relieve her majesty's government from diplomatic difficulties and heavy expenditure," the Colonial Secretary explained.

Soon even *The Times* was singing Rhodes' praises. An editorial pointed out that the company "ought to be able to draw into its nets most of what is worth having in Central Africa."

"As a socio-economic system, British imperialism never got off the ground. As political doctrine it was, for a time, very nearly irresistible." *John Marlowe: Rhodes.*

"Rhodes is my man. His ideas are federation, expansion and consolidation of the Empire." *W. T. Stead—Journalist and Editor*

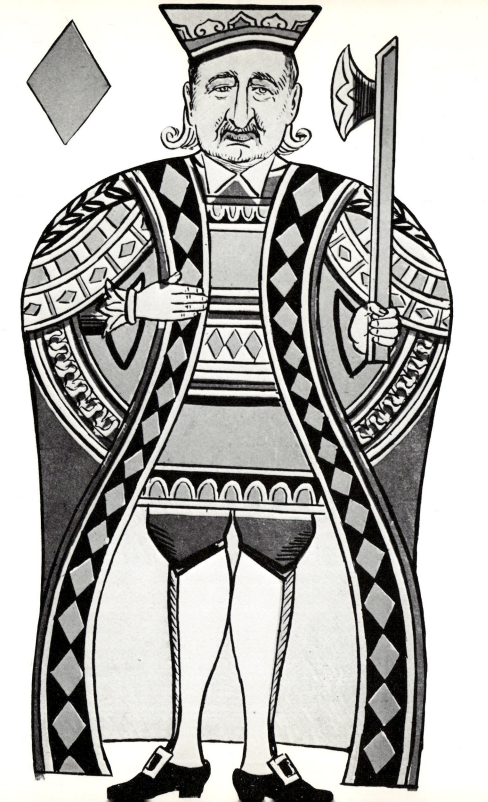

48

Perhaps because of the interest the press had shown Rhodes found himself in great demand. He was invited to many dinner parties and receptions; the other guests were all agog to meet that "extraordinary fellow over from South Africa." Rhodes hated all the wining and dining; "I see no reason to make my interior a dustbin for anyone," he remarked.

But in October, 1889, the charter was signed. The directors included, besides Rhodes and Alfred Beit, two lords and the grandson of a previous British prime minister. Now that Rhodes' British South Africa Company had come into existence, the powers it was given were almost unlimited. It could "make treaties, promulgate laws, preserve the peace, maintain a police force, and acquire new concessions ... make roads, railways, harbours or undertake other public works, own or charter ships, engage in mining or any other industry, establish banks, make land grants, and carry on any lawful commerce, trade pursuit or business." This was a far cry from what Lobengula thought he had agreed to!

There was no defined northern limit to these activities. Rhodes was determined that the way north should be kept open. Whatever Lobengula's thoughts might be the British were content. *The Times* got carried away in its descriptions of the newly acquired territory—"it is rich, fabulously rich, we are told in precious metals and half a dozen others besides" and is "three times the size of the United Kingdom." The area the company now controlled was, in effect, a new colony, and most people were only too pleased to see such an addition to the British Empire.

Left The King of Diamonds.

"... everyone, even, to [Rhodes'] special gratification, the London bus-drivers (whom he regarded as public opinion par excellence), were talking of him and his plans. He was only thirty-six and already had done great things." *Lockhart and Woodhouse: Rhodes.*

9. The Pioneers

> "I made the seizure of the interior the paramount thing in my politics and made everything else subordinate . . . I knew that Africa was the last uncivilized portion of the world, and that it must be civilized, and that those who lived at the healthy base, with the energy that they possess, would be the right and proper individuals to undertake the civilization of the back-country . . ."
>
> *Cecil Rhodes*

When Rhodes returned to Africa he was impatient to get things moving. His interests now included the new railway that ran as far as Kimberley, and he wanted to see this pushing northwards as quickly as possible. He had to be the first into Central Africa. Germany and Portugal who had colonies on the west and east coasts of Africa were already interested in the area and if they beat him to it he felt all would be lost.

Rhodes started to look around for likely young men to join the expedition he was planning to send in to open up the country. There was no shortage of volunteers. He approached Frank Johnston, a man who had a good deal of experience of frontier life behind him, and knew the interior well. Rhodes was impressed with Johnston and felt he would be an asset to the company. "How many men would he need, to make a success of the expedition?" Rhodes asked. "Why," Johnston replied, "with 250 men I would go anywhere in Africa." Rhodes: "That's splendid, you are quite right . . . I appoint you to command the expedition. When will you start?"

But Frank Johnston was not a man to be hurried. He disliked the speed at which Rhodes worked and would not agree to join him until December, 1889, after a good deal of argument. When Rhodes finally persuaded him to accept the young man was full of confidence; "Look here," he said to Rhodes, "you give me a cheque for £94,000 and I will hand your country over to you fit for civil government." Rhodes was satisfied. Very soon enthusiastic volunteers were assembling at Mafeking. Among those eager for the great adventure were farmers, engineers, miners, doctors, builders, lawyers and soldiers. Also included were cricketers, three parsons and a Jesuit!

In Bulawayo, Lobengula was having second thoughts about the whole thing. He was sure he had only given Rhodes' company permission to "dig one hole." But as Lobengula had always insisted that his kingdom included all the lands his warriors raided, Rhodes was in turn convinced this gave the company the right to Mashonaland even further to the north. Now that he had a foothold in Lobengula's kingdom he believed he would have no problem in extending the company's influence.

Left South African "Cape Boys" bound for the gold fields.

Above **Dr Leander Starr Jameson.**

Dr Leander Jameson, as a representative of the South Africa Company, visited the King at Bulawayo before the expedition started. A few miners who had already been sent north to prospect for gold had found nothing and Jameson wanted the King's permission to explore further afield. Lobengula, when told of the plan for the pioneer force, at first objected. But Jameson finally managed to persuade the King to allow the miners to head north-eastwards for Mashonaland and look for gold there. A wary Jameson later confronted the King and asked him whether he intended going back on his word. "The King never lies," said the Matabele chief.

On 27th June, 1890, the pioneers, numbering about one thousand, started on their 450 mile journey. Only two-hundred of these men were white. The remainder included the British South Africa Company's newly formed police force, under the command of Lt Colonel E. G. Pennefather. Along with eighty ox-wagons, the expedition also took enough Maxim machine guns to deal with the Matabele in case they went back on their word and attacked. They were well prepared for life in the bush. In addition to all the usual items such a pioneer force would need, they took with them a complete saw-mill!

When the pioneers reached the border of Matabeleland they received a message from Lobengula who was worried about the size of the expedition. "Has the king killed any white men that an impi is collecting on his border?" he queried. Jameson, who was travelling with the pioneers, replied "These men are a working party, protected by some soldiers and are going along the [route] already arranged with the king."

They pushed on by a roundabout route towards Mashonaland, through, as one put it, "the impenetrable dense and heavy bush . . . and the seemingly endless number of big rivers over which a possible bridge had to be found—often at the cost of a big detour." As this was

> "What incentives . . . the smell of the veldt, the illicit delight of a sabre-slash in the sunshine, a drumbeat out of the forested hills . . . the dull gleam of a nugget in the clay." *James Morris: Pax Britannica.*

the dry season, it is difficult to imagine what hazards they would have encountered later in the year. In August they reached flat, open country where there was less likelihood of ambush. A month later they entered Mashona territory and at long last felt safe from Matabele warriors. Whenever they approached a Mashona village the inhabitants fled on sight. They must have looked quite a formidable army.

The pioneer force had arrived safely—Lobengula had kept his word. They took possession of the territory in Queen Victoria's name. The Union Jack was run up and a salvo of guns fired in celebration. One of the first things they did was to build a fort, which they called Fort Salisbury after the British Prime Minister. The pioneers were extremely pleased with themselves for few white men had previously penetrated so far. "The country's magnificent," one said. They believed they saw signs of gold and other minerals and lost no time in sending a message to Rhodes telling him of their arrival. Settlement could now begin.

As soon as the good news reached civilization, the value of the company's shares shot up on the Stock Exchange. Rhodes was delighted. "When at last I found that they were through to Fort Salisbury, I do not think there was a happier man in the country," he commented.

Above **The Marquis of Salisbury (1830–1903). British Prime Minister (1885–1886, 1886–1892, 1895–1902).**

10. Prime Minister of the Cape

"I like to know how a person votes—not I hasten to say, for any ulterior purpose..." Cecil Rhodes

Below **Cecil Rhodes.**

Rhodes had been eager to accompany the pioneers on their journey, but had decided against it when, in May, 1890, political events had taken a turn for the worse. Prime Minister Sprigg was back in office and had put forward another of his seemingly unworkable ideas—to spend more than seven and a half million pounds building a complicated railway system. Rhodes realized the value of railway communications, but he was not prepared to allow a wasteful programme to be accepted by Parliament. Busy with company affairs, Rhodes had allowed his political activities to take a back seat, but now he dropped everything and hurried to take his seat in the Cape Parliament. There, he joined other opponents to the proposal, and Sprigg was forced to resign yet again.

A new Prime Minister had to be found quickly. The new Governor, Sir Henry Loch, offered the position to Rhodes. He felt that the country needed someone who had the confidence of Hofmeyr and the other leading Boers, and the personality to hold a government together. Rhodes hesitated. He was at first unwilling to take on such a demanding position when his plans for the extension of the Empire already demanded his full attention. But as no other suitable candidates were put forward he finally accepted. "I thought of the positions occupied by De Beers and the Chartered Company, and I concluded that one position could be worked with the other and each to the benefit of all," he wrote.

Once in office, he immediately put his mind to the task in hand, forming a Cabinet of extremely able men, later called the "Cabinet of all the Talents."

Now that he was in power, Rhodes re-emphasised what he wanted to see happen in South Africa—"the expansion of the Cape Colony to the Zambesi" was how he put it. Rhodes' dream of a united South Africa, with no friction between Boer and Briton, appealed to Hofmeyr and his friends. Although many of them would have liked to see this happen under a Boer government, for the moment they were content to back Rhodes, whose plan was to ensure a "government of South Africa by the people of South Africa with the Imperial Flag for defence."

By "the people of South Africa" Rhodes meant blacks as well as whites. His empire-building activities had not led him into racialism, into judging a man harshly because of the colour of his skin. He felt that although the native Africans had the same potential as whites they were not yet politically sophisticated enough to handle their own affairs in a developing territory with any degree of success. In this, too, Rhodes had a sense of mission. "The natives are children and we ought to do something for the minds and brains that the Almighty has given them. I do not believe that they are different from ourselves," he said in Parliament. They would have to be guided until they were politically mature enough to contribute to the running of the country he said, and demanded "equal rights for all civilized men, irrespective of race, south of the Zambesi." Rhodes saw it as part of the European's destiny to pass on his civilization and values to the African and gradually integrate him into the country's political and business life.

"If you cannot manage a thing one way, try another." *Cecil Rhodes*

"If you are really one who loves the natives you must make them worthy of the country they live in, or else you are certain, by an inexorable law, to lose their country. You will certainly not make them worthy if you allow them to sit in idleness and if you do not train them in the arts of civilization." *Cecil Rhodes, 1894.*

"I could never accept the position that we should disqualify a man on account of his colour." *Cecil Rhodes*

Above "Groote Schuur" the one time home of Cecil Rhodes bequeathed by him to the state as the residence of the Premier.

Ever since his arrival in Africa, Rhodes had not had a settled home. Now that he was Prime Minister he decided he should have a house that fitted his position. He found the perfect property on the outskirts of Cape Town. "Groote Schuur," as it was called, suited him ideally. It was a large, simple house, which Rhodes repaired and furnished with country antiques instead of the elaborate furniture of the time. He also built up a fine library of which he was very proud. It included innumerable books on the history and exploration of Africa, together with volumes on mining and politics. He also had a collection of religious and philosophical works. Although Rhodes was of no particular faith himself he was a "religious" man—"let a man be a Buddhist, let him be a Mahommedan, let him be a Christian or what you will, but if he does not believe in a Supreme Being he is no better than a dog," he said.

At "Groote Schuur" he developed a great interest in fruit farming and stock breeding, and had his own private zoo. Although fond of animals he did not appreciate pets, only animals which were useful in some way. "I invited you to dinner, but not your infernal dog," he snapped at a guest who had brought his house dog with him.

Rhodes believed in an easy-going life style, and at his house he had the opportunity of living exactly as he wanted. There were always plenty of visitors, not just politicians and business acquaintances, but farmers, hunters, miners and anybody else who had a good story to tell. Rhodes enjoyed talking, and liked to go riding with a few companions whilst discussing a wide variety of subjects.

He was not the easiest man to make a friend of, and appeared cold and aloof to many people, particularly in public. In the privacy of his own home however, he became almost a different person. One guest said of him, "It has been my lot during a long life to converse with some of the most distinguished talkers of the day. I must say that, in my opinion, Cecil Rhodes would have been hard to beat when he was at home. . . . There were powers of thought, originality of expression, and more humour than those who knew him slightly were ready to credit."

Rhodes was content in his new home. It was a place where he could collect his thoughts, plan his next course of action and meet and talk with people who were not out to impress him or gain a favour. It gave him a breathing space away from the activity of his business and political life.

> "You often speak more freely at your dining-table than you would in public, because you do not expect what you say to be reported." *Cecil Rhodes*

> "He does not want any living man to know him. His life and interests seem mapped out into squares; and the man who is concerned with Square 6 must know nothing of Square 7." *H. L. Currey—one-time Secretary to Rhodes*

11. Matabele War

Now, for the first time, Cecil Rhodes visited his new country. It was already being called Rhodesia, and he accepted the compliment as his right. In October, 1891, he arrived in Fort Salisbury, only to hear that the settlers were discontented. Their hopes of vast gold deposits were fading fast, only small quantities had been found. The rainy season had been much worse than expected and it had been impossible to grow anything successfully. Some settlers had already died of starvation, and many who had arrived after the pioneers had given up and gone home.

There were as yet no real communications in the new country. Rhodes was striving to push the railway and telegraph up from the south as fast as possible, and he promised the settlers that food supplies would be brought in and everything possible done to make the venture a success. To him it was unthinkable that his country would not succeed. To cut costs much of the police force was disbanded and settlers were supplied with guns in order to defend themselves against possible native raids. When the rains finished new settlers started to appear on the scene. They brought with them up-to-date mining equipment and other sorely needed supplies, including ample quantities of whisky!

But the Matabele were still a force to be reckoned with, although Rhodes did not expect any real trouble from Lobengula as yet.

Then in May, 1893, one of those small things that give rise to significant events occurred. Five-hundred yards of wire from the newly built telegraph were cut down and stolen. The Mashona liked using this wire to make bracelets and other articles. A chief called Gomala was thought to be the culprit. When company police arrived at his kraal he duly paid his fine in cattle. The only problem was they were not his to give away! They belonged to Lobengula. The King complained and his cattle were returned. But the damage had been done. Lobengula decided to show the Mashona what he thought of cattle thieves.

In July the Matabele entered Mashonaland in force. Although they had been ordered not to touch the settlers' property, in their warlike mood they set upon Mashona servants and stole cattle. Everyone who could scrambled to get into the local company fort for protection. One of Lobengula's officers, Manyao, went to the fort and demanded that the Mashona hiding there should be given up. This request was refused.

A meeting was arranged between the settlers and the Matabele, and the white men insisted that the warriors go back to Bulawayo. The main body did, but some of the more warlike young men refused to go. They continued looting, so a party of thirty-eight mounted white men were sent against them. The Matabele were attacked as they were preparing to steal more cattle from a Mashona village. The warriors fled, leaving about forty men dead.

Lobengula had not intended that his men should steal cattle themselves. After all, they had been sent to punish those who had stolen his. But when his army returned, he saw how his warriors had been humiliated and he decided not to return the cattle. Furthermore, he demanded that the original Mashona culprits be handed over to him for punishment. The settlers were by now in no mood to agree to such a demand and were deter-

"So long as the Matabele do not molest my people I cannot declare war on them; but as soon as they interfere with our rights I shall certainly end their game." *Cecil Rhodes.*

mined to crush the Matabele, "now and forever" as one put it. In August they set about raising a volunteer force to fight the Matabele. As payment the men were to receive 6,000 acres of land, twenty gold claims and a share of any loot they might lay their hands on. Command was given to Major Patrick Forbes. The force consisted of six-hundred white men, four-hundred native soldiers, five Maxim guns and a few field guns.

Although Lobengula's warriors, for their part, were eager to make up for their defeat, the King decided to have one last try at averting the conflict by sending three envoys to Cape Town, at the request of the High Commissioner, to work out an agreement. On the way two were killed by police who thought hostilities had started and attempted to arrest them. The third returned to Lobengula with his sad tale. "The white men are the fathers of lies," raged the King. It was the end of the road. His army went out to meet the volunteers.

Below On the road to the front in Matabeleland: refugees coming on foot from Bulawayo in 1896.

Major Forbes' force, together with 1,500 Bechuana warriors, traditional enemies of the Matabele, marched towards Bulawayo. They crossed the Shangani river on 24th October and camped for the night. The Matabele attacked in the early morning. They were beaten back twice by the white men's artillery, and then came on again with desperate courage. But they were no match for the volunteers secure behind their camp wall. Although the Matabele had guns they did not know how to use them effectively. By 9.30 that morning it was all over. The Matabele had lost six hundred men. The Europeans had hardly any casualties.

Throughout the following week the Company's men continued their advance until they came to another river—the Imbembesi, where, after striking camp, they saw no less than 7,000 Matabele warriors advancing towards them through the bush. The Matabele attacked the camp with great bravery and determination, as

Below A dramatic scene from the Matabele War.

Above Volunteers in action in the Matabele War.

befitted the cream of Lobengula's army. Again they stood no chance against the enemy's superior firepower, and after two more attempts were forced to retreat, losing many of their number.

The Company column moved on to Bulawayo with no opposition. When they arrived they found that Lobengula, his wives and remaining warriors had fled. His kraal had been blown up with gunpowder. The volunteers marched in to the sound of bagpipes, and to their surprise found two white men still alive among the ruins. The King had personally protected them while his warriors were trying to destroy the white army.

Patrols were sent out to find Lobengula with no success. One, led by Major Allan Wilson with twenty-one troopers, was completely wiped out by Lobengula's warriors when they stumbled on the King and his men in the bush. But Lobengula was not even to enjoy this small victory for long. In 1894 he died, probably of smallpox. Before he died he told his people to seek protection from Rhodes, "He will be your chief and your friend," he said.

The Matabele chiefs sued for peace. They were told to hand over their weapons and were allowed to return to their villages. The Company's volunteers were given the farms and mining claims they had been promised. "It is your right for you have conquered the country," said Rhodes.

Back in Cape Town Rhodes found himself fighting against several opponents of what had happened in Matabeleland. But when the full story of events became known opinion swung in Rhodes' favour and they found themselves outnumbered. People began to feel that winning the country with a handful of men was something to be proud of. Compared to other wars in Africa it had certainly been both quick and cheap.

Lobengula's sons appear to have been rather young, and there were no other obvious successors to the King. Now there was nothing to stop expansion into the territory of the leaderless Matabele. A town grew up at Bulawayo, and the country was integrated with Mashonaland for administrative convenience. Soon would-be farmers were streaming into the country. Miners arrived too, after all, massive gold deposits might be found in the old King's land! Rhodesia was fast becoming a reality!

"Rebellion against an armed opposition to British rule had been a characteristic of the British Empire in one part or another, throughout most of its history." *Colin Cross: The Fall of the British Empire.*

12. The Jameson Raid

Cecil Rhodes was riding on the crest of a wave, Rhodesia was thriving; he was Prime Minister of Cape Colony and one of the richest men in the world. His interests included the main telegraph company in South Africa, the railways, and he also owned several newspapers. During a visit to Britain in 1894 Rhodes had even been invited to dine with Queen Victoria at Windsor Castle. The Queen was very pleased at the additions he had made to her Empire. They are reported to have had the following conversation—Queen Victoria: "What have you been doing since I last saw you, Mr. Rhodes?" Rhodes: "I have added two Provinces to Your Majesty's dominions." It seemed as if nothing could affect his success. But storm clouds were gathering on the horizon.

The men who had come to the Transvaal to dig for gold, Britons, other Europeans, and Americans, were discontended. Kruger, now in his sixties, had been elected for the third time and was determined the "Uitlanders" (outlanders or foreigners) as the miners were called, should have no say in the government of his country. He refused to give them the vote even though they were forced to pay vast taxes. Most had, of course, come to the Rand simply to make money. While they were busy prospecting they were reasonably content and did not concern themselves about politics. But, in 1894, there was a slump and they began to suspect that they were being exploited by the Boers. Kruger appears to

> "If I were President Kruger, I might not have given the Uitlanders the franchise, because that might have ended my power. But I would have made my new population comfortable and given them justice." *Cecil Rhodes.*

Above left Workers from the Grahamstown Gold Mining Company, 1888.

Below left Workers from the Republic Gold Mining Company, 1888.

have been very narrow-minded; perhaps a more far-sighted person would have realized what could happen with such a large number of resentful people in the country. But Kruger considered that they were not worth bothering about. The President called them "thieves and murderers" and said, "I shall never give them anything. I shall never change my policy." The Uitlanders felt it was time they took things into their own hands. Revolution was in the air.

Cecil Rhodes was fascinated by these rumours of revolution. In May, 1895, he met with two of the Uitlander ringleaders in Cape Town to discuss how he could help, and decided to back the revolt. At once he set about smuggling arms and ammunition into Johannesburg. Jameson was told to raise a volunteer force in the Colony ready to support the rising. Also involved in the intrigue was Colonel Francis (Frank) Rhodes, brother of Cecil Rhodes and an officer in the 1st Dragoons. He was staying in the colony and it was thought that his military experience might be useful. Rhodes and the Colonial Secretary, Joseph Chamberlain, who knew about the plot, were anxious for the rebellion to begin as soon as possible. The plotters began to have doubts. Perhaps just the threat of a revolt would be enough to get Kruger to change his ideas? Was it worth risking all in an uprising? The non-British were worried that Rhodes was only backing them because he wanted to bring the Transvaal under the British flag. The conspirators decided to postpone the rising until they were more sure of themselves—and Rhodes.

Meanwhile, Jameson and his men were growing increasingly impatient for action. The Doctor was confident he would have no problem in defeating Kruger and settling the problem. He paraded his troops and informed them they had been invited into the Transvaal by oppressed immigrants. His men were enthusiastic and felt ready for anything. In Cape Town Rhodes had been

Below Joseph Chamberlain (1836–1914), British Colonial Secretary from 1895 to 1903.

told the rebellion was off, at least for the time being. He sent a telegram post-haste to Jameson saying, "On no account whatever must you move." The telegraph wire had been cut and it is likely that Jameson never received the message. It might not have made much difference if he had. He had already decided on his plan of attack.

On 29th December, 1895, the raiders rode out, two columns strong, to teach Kruger a lesson. They were sure they were doing the right thing. 372 men, a field gun and six Maxims made up the first detachment, 122 men, two field guns and two Maxims made up the second. The two columns joined up at Malmani near the border and crossed into the Transvaal. They were continually watched by armed Boers as they cantered towards Johannesburg. The band headed into hilly country, dogged by a watchful enemy who started to take potshots at them. The raiders marched towards

Below Incriminating evidence against Jameson: fragments of a letter sent by Colonel Francis Rhodes, Cecil's brother, picked up at Doornkop after the Raid.

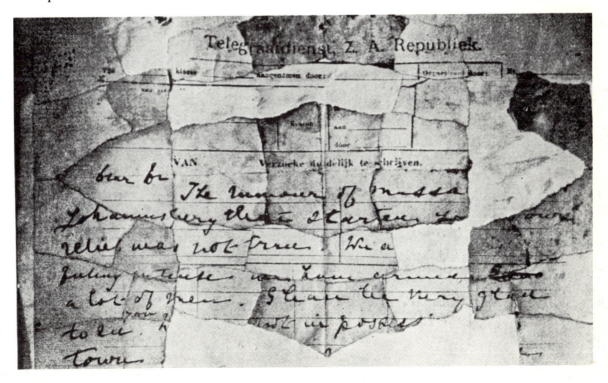

Krugersdorp about twenty miles from Johannesburg but the Boers were ready for them. Jamesons's force bombarded the enemy defences with field guns and then advanced at the double, only to be surprised by a Boer detachment which appeared at their rear. Finding themselves surrounded, they moved south trying to find a way out of the trap and heard the sound of gunfire in the distance. Sure that a party of Uitlanders had arrived from Johannesburg to help, they took new heart. They were tragically wrong. These were Boer reinforcements that had arrived on the scene. The trapped raiders who had been on the march for three days, were worn out and had no food. They made camp for the night and suffered under continual sniping from Boer commandos.

Below Jameson's last stand, 2nd January, 1896.

There were already several casualties, but in the morning Jameson attacked once more, and as the Boers began to intensify their fire things went from bad to worse. Jameson was running out of ammunition and many of the Maxims jammed. The raiders, greatly outnumbered, could not advance, and retreat was impossible. On 2nd January they surrendered. What became known as the Jameson Raid had been a fiasco from beginning to end.

Cecil Rhodes was in deep trouble. He could not deny that he had been involved in the affair. All he could say was that he had certainly not given Jameson the order to advance. The British Government had already made it plain they would never admit to any knowledge of the plot. Nor could Rhodes count on Hofmeyr any more. The leader of the Afrikaaner Bond was outraged when he heard the news. "If Rhodes is behind this," he stormed, "he is no more a friend of mine." It was also possible that the Chartered Company would suffer because of Rhodes' part in the plot. For its founder to be involved in an armed raid into the Afrikaaner republic was too much for many people to accept. Although some British people were sympathetic to Rhodes and felt that Jameson had been let down by the Uitlanders, the Prime Minister and his government were forced to resign.

In Johannesburg Kruger was having a field day. He arrested all the Uitlander ringleaders he could trace and started a city-wide search for hidden hoards of guns and ammunition. Union in South Africa was further away than ever.

On 15th January, 1896, Rhodes boarded a ship for England. In February he had an interview with Joseph Chamberlain. Unfortunately, there is no record of what passed between them but obviously Rhodes came out on top again. The Chartered Company was safe.

"I do not think he slept for five nights. Tony, his personal servant, told me 'The Baas walks up and down his bedroom, which is locked, at all times of the night." *Rhodes' Secretary, Philip Jourdan, describing Rhodes' reaction to the Jameson Raid.*

Below The Parliamentary Inquiry into the Jameson Raid. Mr Cecil Rhodes giving evidence before the South Africa Committee, *The Illustrated London News,* 27th February, 1897.

As to Jameson's fate he and his officers were sent to London for trial. Rhodes paid for their defence and they received light sentences. He also arranged for the release of other plotters held in the Transvaal by paying heavy fines to Kruger on their behalf. Colonel Frank Rhodes lost his commission but recovered it in time to serve in the Boer War, notably at the Seige of Ladysmith.

Below Jameson (centre) with his officers who took part in the Raid photographed aboard ship on their return to England, 1898.

13. Rhodes the Peacemaker

Cecil Rhodes was no longer Prime Minister of the Cape and had been within a hairsbreadth of complete ruin. Intent on leaving failure behind, he set out for Rhodesia. But here, too, the situation had taken a turn for the worse. The Matabele were restive. Many members of the Company's police force had left to take part in the Jameson Raid, and there were only hastily organized units of volunteers to keep the peace. The tribesmen were annoyed at the way they were treated by those in authority, and particularly at the remedy chosen to combat a serious outbreak of cattle disease. To prevent it spreading the Company administration insisted on slaughtering great numbers of cattle. The Matabele felt bitter about this as the animals were their principal form of wealth. When news of the Jameson Raid reached their villages they realized that while the white men were fighting amongst themselves it was an ideal time to take revenge. Urged on by their witch-doctors they struck in March, 1896, attacking outlying settler farms and killing many of the inhabitants.

Rhodes reached Salisbury just as the seriousness of the situation was becoming apparent. He immediately started to organize relief columns for the threatened areas. Regular army officers were brought in to command the forces available, including Colonel Baden-Powell, who was later to found the Boy Scout Movement. Rhodes applied himself to the hostilities with

"The few who knew him loved him. The majority, to whom he was unknown, paid him their homage, some of their admiration, and others of their hate. And it must be admitted that the dread he inspired among those who disliked him was more widespread than the affection he commanded from those who came within the magic of his presence." *W. T. Stead—Journalist and Editor*

Below The Brothers Rhodes in 1896—Cecil on the left and Francis (1851–1905) on the right.

enthusiasm and when Bulawayo was relieved in June he rode in with the soldiers. Fighting still continued, however. It began to look impossible for the whites to bring things to a satisfactory conclusion. After a defeat the Matabele simply melted away, only to reappear next day ready for another battle. To make matters worse the hitherto meek Mashona also rose in rebellion.

Against the advice of the professional soldiers in command, Rhodes decided to meet the Matabele and try and reach a settlement without further bloodshed. After many fruitless attempts he managed to convince the Matabele chiefs of his sincerity. A meeting was arranged in the Matopo Hills, south of Bulawayo. Rhodes went unarmed, with only a handful of men. The group was immediately surrounded by hostile warriors. He went in amongst them alone, arguing with the younger and

Below Cecil Rhodes meets the Matabele chiefs in the Matopo Hills, 1896.

more aggressive chiefs who were eager to continue the fighting. The older men, tired of war, sided with Rhodes, and the talking began. The Matabele had many complaints. They said the treatment they received from the settlers was worse than they would give their own dogs. The chiefs insisted that the officials set over them were corrupt, and grumbled that they had to pay excessive taxes. Rhodes saw that their complaints were justified, and continued the talks with understanding and patience. When he pointed out that it had been wrong of them to kill European women and children, he was immediately informed by Somabulane, a Matabele chief, that the settlers had murdered Matabele women and children first. This was unfortunately true, the Matabele certainly had not been treated honourably. Rhodes set about solving the problems.

In October a final meeting was held and peace terms agreed. Rhodes arranged for 4,500 bags of maize to be distributed to the Matabele, who had been unable to plant crops during the war and were nearing starvation. He also promised that new Company officials would be brought in to run the country. The tomb of Lobengula's father, badly damaged by British troops, was repaired, and Rhodes saw that the culprits were punished. Once the Matabele had come to an agreement the hostile Mashona, too, lay down their arms. Peace was restored.

Rhodes, now a private citizen with a personal income of £$\frac{1}{2}$ million per annum, devoted himself to developing the land he had won. He financed more railways and telegraph lines, set up factories and farms, and even introduced ladybirds into the country to protect the orange trees from greenfly. He still found time for long trips through the bush—hunting and shooting, or leisurely talking with his companions. It was a good time, but it could not last.

Early in 1898, Rhodes returned to the Cape and found himself involved in politics again. His handling of the

"By the end of June the rebellion had been contained. Bulawayo, which a month before had been virtually in a state of siege, had been relieved. Matabele concentrations near the European settlements had been dispersed, and communications between the principal towns restored. But the Matabele, in their fastnessess had not been defeated." *John Marlowe: Cecil Rhodes: The Anatomy of Empire.*

Right Cecil Rhodes.

Matabele uprising had regained him some of the old favour. He spoke out for union in South Africa and spent much time attacking Kruger. He was re-elected at Barkly West, even though there was increasing discord between Boer and Briton in the Colony. For a time it looked as if he might reach the top of the political ladder again. But this renewed interest in politics was not to last for he found Cape affairs tame compared to what he felt he could achieve in the north. At the end of December he sailed for England to discuss business and finalize plans for the further development of his railway and telegraph.

14. The Siege of Kimberley

In July, 1899, Rhodes boarded ship for Cape Town after six months discussing business in England. In South Africa the rift between Boers and British had been widening. The grievances of the Uitlanders were no nearer solution. Kruger was convinced that if he gave them the vote they would end up running his country. Many possible solutions had been put forward during the past year but none that would give the Uitlanders what they wanted, and at the same time make sure the Transvaal remained under Boer control. Kruger was not prepared to put up with any more British attempts to solve the problem, and spoke out against "the insolent demands of the British Government." In October Boer forces moved across the border from the Transvaal and Orange Free State into Natal and Cape Colony. The inevitable had taken place.

Rhodes was on his way to Kimberley when war broke out. His train arrived there on the 11th. He only just made it. Soon the town was surrounded by swarms of Boers. Although troops were stationed in Kimberley, under the command of Lieutenant Colonel Robert Kekewich, a little-known officer in the army, the citizens felt very vulnerable. Although the Boers would probably never have succeeded in storming Kimberley (they had neither the equipment or the skill), there was still a great

"Kruger's troops were unlike any others in the world. Apart from one or two commanders and the regular artillery, they had learnt little of military science. They lacked text-book knowledge, but they had an abundance of common sense. They were frontier men, with frontiermen's skills: good shots, hard riders and above all masters of terrain." *Brian Gardner: The Lion's Cage.*

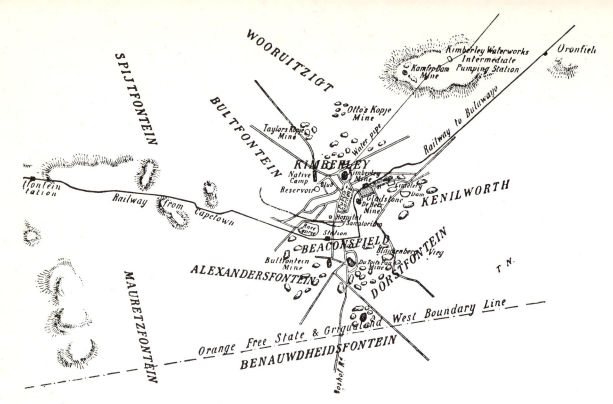

Above A map of Kimberley and surrounding districts.

"There is no fear of our surrendering, but we are getting anxious about the state of the British Army. It is high time you did something." *Cecil Rhodes in a message to Lord Roberts*

sense of danger. For these farmers were both tough and courageous, and they soon succeeded in making a nuisance of themselves. Boer guns were moved onto a ridge just outside the town. At first the shelling was simply inconvenient. Most damage was to property. One shell went right through a hotel where people were having lunch and ended up in the pantry. The only casualties were two dead cats and some broken cups and saucers. *The Daily Telegraph* commented that the inhabitants "looked upon the shelling much as they would have done upon a firework display." But the bombardment became more severe and soon Kimberley was suffering attack every day except Sunday.

In addition to the bombardment, it was impossible for supplies to get through the Boer lines. Morale was low and food was running out. Cats and dogs were caught in the streets and taken home to be cooked and eaten. Horses were served up in stews and casseroles.

Eggs cost £1.00 a dozen. It was impossible to obtain fresh vegetables, and people were reduced to eating garden weeds!

Rhodes had no confidence in Kekewich and was determined to take things into his own hands. He behaved very badly to the Colonel, and insulted him to his face in public. But without Rhodes the plight of everyone might have been much worse. He helped form a special committee to investigate any hardship that the families of men killed or wounded had to face. The tunnels and mine-shafts were converted into shelters for the women and children when the town was being

"You are afraid of a mere handful of farmers armed with rifles. You call yourself soldiers of an Empire-making nation. I do believe you will next take fright at a pair of broomsticks dressed up in trousers." *Rhodes to Kekewich*

Below A dug out shelter, West End Kimberley.

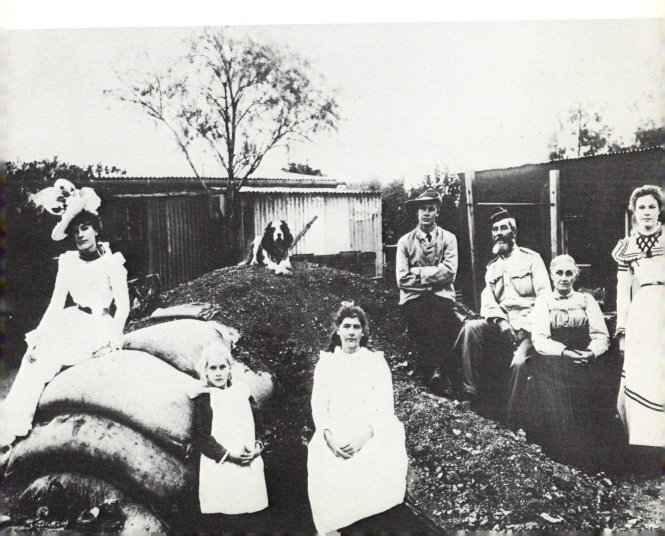

shelled, and Rhodes arranged for the De Beers Company workshops to manufacture guns and ammunition, using Boer shells that had landed in the town as the raw material. George Labram, one of Rhodes' engineers, went to work and designed a particularly large gun. "Long Cecil", as it was called, went into action on 19th January, 1900.

On 24th January the worst shelling the town had as yet suffered began. It continued without let up for two days. One eye-witness said, "We had a pretty hot time . . . the unmistakeable 'whiz' of a shell, followed at once by its explosion, let me know that trouble was mighty near."

Hope of relief was fading. On 7th February a new Boer weapon appeared on the scene, a gun that was far more powerful than anything they had used before. The first shell started a large fire in the town centre, but the fire service managed to stop it spreading. Shell splinters killed a baby in its mother's arms and a barman was decapitated whilst serving drinks. But relief was, in fact, on the way. Huge clouds of dust could be seen in the distance and the sound of gunfire reached the town. The relief column of British troops had arrived. On 15th February Kimberley was relieved by a force of 25,000 men led by General John French. The siege had lasted 124 days.

Rhodes held a celebration dinner for the officers. He produced champagne and other delicacies which he had kept for just such an occasion. Rather surprising when people had been living on horse meat and other unsavoury items for months!

"Kimberley is won, Mr Cecil Rhodes is free, the De Beers' shareholders are all full of themselves, and the beginning of the war is at an end. It is a great feat to have accomplished, and the happiest omen for the future." *The Daily Mail 17/2/1900*

"The most marvellous thing about England is her luck. We have made the silliest mistake, we have some of the most incompetant generals, but we are coming out all right, as we always do." *Cecil Rhodes, quoted in The Daily Mail, 17th March, 1900.*

"We have done our best to preserve that which is the best commercial asset in the world, the protection of Her Majesty's flag." *Cecil Rhodes after the relief of Kimberley*

Far left above Rhodes with the gun called "Long Cecil" at the siege of Kimberley during the Boer War.

Far left below Fortifications in Kimberley during the siege 1899–1900.

15. "So much to do . . ."

What was to be known as the Boer War lasted for almost three years, but Rhodes, now back at the Cape, found himself side-tracked by a Princess. The divorced wife of a Russian aristocrat, the clever, witty, unscrupulous Princess Radziwill. Rhodes had known her for some time and she was frequently a dinner guest at Groote Schuur. But now the Princess was fast becoming a nuisance. She had begun to meddle in Rhodes' affairs and tried to worm her way into his affections. The Princess had definite ideas about the course of Rhodes' career and attempted to pressurize him into becoming Prime Minister of the Cape again. Pretending to be a great friend of Lord Salisbury, the British Prime Minister, she insisted that he too was eager for Rhodes to take up the position once more. Rhodes, however, knew his own mind which was dwelling increasingly on the trouble in the north. He had lost his enthusiasm for party politics. His health was beginning to worry him, but he believed he could count on a few more years of life. To escape from the Princess he decided to go travelling and hunting in Rhodesia for a few months, although he would have to return to Cape Town later in the year for a long-standing engagement.

On his return to Cape Town in October Rhodes made it quite clear that he no longer wished to be involved in

Above Cecil Rhodes pictured in later life.

Cape politics. He bought a Wolseley motor car, then a great novelty, and went for drives in the countryside and discussed the idea of a world tour with Alfred Beit. He also spent much time planning his will. Then in March, 1901, tired of the rather lazy life he had been leading, Rhodes decided to go first to Kimberley and Bulawayo, and then take a shooting holiday in Scotland, stopping off in London to visit a heart specialist. The news was not good. Rhodes, although only forty-eight years old, was seriously ill and was told that under no circumstances should he continue living at the hectic pace which had so distinguished his life. The Scottish holiday helped. He was joined by Jameson, Beit and Philip Jourdon his secretary. The young Winston Churchill also stayed at the hunting lodge for a short spell, where, with the group of friends, he—"rode ponies and carried guns and engaged in various affairs, nominally sporting."

Meanwhile back in Cape Town, the Princess was very busy, but she was also broke and in great need of money. Some historians think it possible that she had got hold of some compromising papers about the Jameson Raid and was attempting to blackmail Rhodes. We do know that she spread rumours around town to the effect that she was Rhodes' mistress and that he visited her regularly in her bedroom. Whether there was any truth in these tales or not, the Princess does not seem to have been very successful in getting money out of Rhodes by this means, as she ended up by forging his signature on a cheque for £4,500 and falsifying other documents to obtain large sums of money in his name.

Below The arrest of Princess Radziwill on a charge of forging Cecil Rhodes' name—as reported in the newspapers in February, 1902.

THE RADZIWILL CASE.

ARREST OF THE PRINCESS ON A FORGERY CHARGE.

CAPETOWN, Wednesday, Feb. 26.

Princess Radziwill was arrested this morning on a charge of forging the name of Mr. Cecil Rhodes to certain bills, which formed the subject of recent legal proceedings, wherein Mr. Rhodes swore that the signatures were not his.

By January, 1902, when Rhodes was back in London, the situation at the Cape was quite out of hand. T. J. Louw, an old acquaintance of Rhodes', had cashed a cheque for the Princess and now decided to take legal action to recover his money. The trouble maker was arrested and Rhodes was asked to return to appear at the investigation. He arrived in South Africa in February. The day after his arrival in South Africa, Rhodes appeared before a commission and stated that the signatures on all documents in question were not his. Although Rhodes had no further contact with his former friend, the trouble she had caused began to take its toll. The worry of the affair and the sea voyage had

> "The world is nearly all parcelled out, and what there is left of it is being divided up, conquered and colonised. To think of these stars that you see overhead at night . . . I would annex the planets if I could—I often think of that." *A statement made by Rhodes towards the end of his life.*

Below Cecil Rhodes on the site of his grave in 1897.

done him no good at all. He had drunk rather too much on the ship, caught a severe chill and had a bad fall one night, none of which was likely to help his worsening heart condition. His increasing ill health forced him to retire to a cottage on the coast. He never appeared in Cape Town again.

It was obvious to everyone but Rhodes that he could not live much longer. He was allowed to receive only good news, and was given a faked edition of the *Cape Argus* which reported that his health was improving. His mind still dwelt on future plans. He ordered a passage booked on a ship to England, and to appease him a cabin was specially prepared. But on the 26th March, 1902, the day the ship sailed, he died. His last words were, "So little done, so much to do." Rhodes was forty-eight.

Below The funeral of Cecil Rhodes: lowering the body into the tomb in the Matapo Hills.

He had requested that his funeral should be, in his own words, "big and simple, barbaric if you like." His body was moved to Groote Schuur, where it lay in state before being taken to Cape Town for the burial service. Afterwards it was placed in Rhodes' recently completed personal train for the journey to Rhodesia, where he wanted to be buried. There were mourners at every halt, including one of Lobengula's sons.

On the 8th April the train reached Bulawayo. The next day the coffin was carried into the Matopo hills, the scene of his historic meeting with the Matabele. Thousands of Matabele warriors lined the route and gave Rhodes the royal salute, *Bayete*, never before given to a white man. Perhaps they felt that, for all his faults, he had been their chief by right of conquest. Together with the bodies of Jameson and those who died in Allan Wilson's ill-fated patrol, the remains of Cecil Rhodes still lie in the heart of Africa.

"He lies buried on the mountain, the lizards crawling over a massive stone lacking any cross or religious symbol. 'A haunted, sinister pagan place,' wrote a British High Commissioner . . ." *Colin Cross: The Fall of the British Empire.*

16. Postscript

"For the future of Rhodesia no longer lies in the hands of the Europeans. It is not a question now of if, but when and how, the Africans will take over. More Africans are born every year than there are European workers in employment. Rhodesia is a pressure cooker with the lid screwed down by the Europeans, and it will blow up in their faces." *John Parker: Rhodesia: Little White Island.*

The present-day image of Cecil Rhodes is one of an imperialist, and the present-day does not take kindly to such men. But perhaps he should not be judged too harshly. Although Rhodes used the usual methods of imperialism, including trickery and the Maxim gun, his aims were more positive than the outright exploitation that motivated many of his contemporaries. In *Pax Britannica* James Morris says of Rhodes, "He really thought of the Empire as an instrument of universal peace. There was nothing niggling in his imperial sentiments." He was genuinely inspired by a vision of the world free from strife, speaking a common language and with every country a vital part of the whole. A worthy ideal, although today we might disagree with the way he tried to realize it. The fact that Rhodes was an Englishman who saw London as the capital of his world state and the Queen at its head does not detract from his breadth of vision. In his attitude to race we have seen that Rhodes displayed a liberal attitude for the time; to him civilized values rather than racial differences were what counted. Rhodes' values were those of a white race convinced that it was God's will that they should govern the less advanced and "pagan" peoples of the world.

Despite the fact that within the framework of his time Rhodes was more far-seeing than most, his dreams have not become realities. In May, 1902, the Boer War came

Above An old French cartoon of Cecil
Rhodes: "Money is other men's
blood."

to an end. A British victory led to the union of Boer
republics and British colonies—the Union of South
Africa. Since that time the rifts in South African society
have become more pronounced. Today it is a land
divided, not simply between those of Dutch and British
ancestry, but between white people and black.
Apartheid (separateness), the law which aims at separate
development for white and black, has led, in practice,
to the indignity of racial segregation in residen-
tial areas, in jobs, on the buses and even on the cricket
field. Cecil Rhodes, although no saint, would probably
have been appalled. Rhodesia, for a long time thought
to be a model multi-racial society is today in an official
state of rebellion against Britain. The colony was due to

Below The Empire was of vital importance during the reign of Queen Victoria and all nations were urged to fight to ensure that South Africa became a part of this Empire.

gain independence from Britain and join Africa's black nations in having a popularly elected government when, in 1965, Rhodesia's Prime Minister, Ian Smith, rebelled and took hold of the reins of power. Since then the rift between Britain and Rhodesia has widened. The Rhodesian way of life seems to be increasingly modelled on Afrikaaner-dominated South Africa. A settlement that will lead to a fair share for all, including black Rhodesians, in governing the country grows more unlikely each year. Unless a solution is reached, it is possible that political extremism will destroy any chance for a just society in the territories Rhodes helped to create.

Although Rhodes' grand plan for Africa ("all that red") did not materialize, his last will shows that he never lost sight of his dream of a world civilized by English-speaking peoples. In it he made provision for scholarships to Oxford University for young men from Canada, Australia, South Africa, Rhodesia, Jamaica, Bermuda and the United States of America. He hoped that during their period of study they would grow to understand and appreciate the benefits of a union between English-speaking nations of the world, and so work towards such a goal.

The scholarships, worth £300 a year for three years, were not to go to those who were "merely bookworms." The perfect candidate would, to quote the will, be judged on:

"1. His literary and scholastic attainments
  2. His fondness for and success in manly outdoor sports such as cricket, football and the like
  3. His qualities of manhood, truth, courage, devotion to duty, sympathy for and protection of the weak, kindliness, unselfishness and fellowship
  4. His exhibition during school days of moral force of character and of instincts to lead and to take an interest in his schoolmates."

Through the scholarships Rhodes has enabled many people to benefit from a university education, and they are a lasting tribute to their founder in a changed world. But, as some biographers point out, Cecil Rhodes himself would never have qualified. Nor would the majority of freebooters, speculators, explorers and soldiers who played a part in this particular adventure.

Principal Characters

Barnato, Barney (1855–1897). Kimberley businessman and speculator. Member of Cape Parliament.

Beit, Alfred (1853–1906). Diamond expert. Arranged financial backing for many of Rhodes' enterprises.

Chamberlain, J. (1836–1914). Achieved fame in 1875 as radical Lord Mayor of Birmingham pioneering slum clearance schemes. He became British Colonial Secretary in 1895. In 1906 he was struck down by paralysis and took no further part in politics.

Gordon, General (1833–1885). Renowned British soldier. Fought in many countries, notably in China (from 1860 to 1865), Sudan. Died in Khartoum after a siege of ten months, two days before the arrival of a relief force.

Hofmeyr, J. (1845–1909). Cape Politician. Leader of the Afrikaaner Bond.

Jameson, Dr L. S. (1853–1917). Friend of Rhodes'. Travelled with the Pioneers and led the Jameson Raid. He served a prison sentence in Britain but later returned to South Africa and was Premier of Cape Colony 1904–8.

Kruger, P. (1825–1904). President of the Transvaal and one of the main political opponents of the British.

Lobengula (*c.* 1832–1894). King of the Matabele.

Radziwill, Princess Catherine (1858–1941). Adventuress and sometime journalist. Convicted of forgery on Rhodes' testimony.

Robinson, Sir H. (1824–1897). British Colonial Administrator in Cape Colony. He also held this post in Hong Kong, Ceylon, New South Wales and the Fiji Islands.

Rudd, Charles (1844–?). Rhodes' friend and partner in the diamond fields.

Salisbury, Lord (1830–1903). British Prime Minister (1885–6; 1886–92; 1895–1902) and Foreign Secretary, 1878–1880.

Sprigg, Gordon (1830–1913). Cape Politician and Prime Minister.

Table of Dates

1853   Birth of Cecil Rhodes.
1870   Rhodes sails for Africa.
1873   Rhodes is accepted as an undergraduate at Oriel College, Oxford.
1878   Rhodes returns to Kimberley to fulfil his ambitions.
1881   Rhodes enters the Cape Parliament.
1888   The concession is gained from Lobengula.
1889   Rhodes' Chartered Company is formed.
1890   The Pioneers set out for Matabeleland. Rhodes becomes Prime Minister of the Cape.
1891   The Matabele War.
1895   The Jameson Raid.
1896   Second Matabele War.
1899   Outbreak of the Boer War. Beginning of the Siege of Kimberley.
1900   Relief of Kimberley.
1902   Rhodes' death. Boer War ends.

Further Reading

Cross, C. *The Fall of the British Empire* (Hodder and Stoughton, 1968). An impartial account of the history of the British Empire and Commonwealth from 1918 to 1966.

Gardner, B. *The Lion's Cage: Cecil Rhodes and the Siege of Kimberley* (Arthur Barker, 1969). The full story of the siege drawn from official and unofficial papers and personal accounts. A unique appraisal of an empire-builder.

Hanna, A. J. *The Story of the Rhodesias and Nyasaland* (Faber and Faber, 1960). An objective account of the Rhodesias and Nyasaland from the middle of the nineteenth century to the middle of the twentieth. Somewhat outdated by recent events.

Lockhart, J. G. and Woodhouse, the Hon. C. M. *Rhodes* (Hodder and Stoughton, 1963). A definitive account of Rhodes' life based on unpublished sources.

Marlowe, J. *Cecil Rhodes: The Anatomy of Empire* (Paul Elek, 1972). An examination of British imperialism through the character of Cecil Rhodes.

Morris, J. *Pax Britannica, The Climax of an Empire* (Faber and Faber, 1968). A detailed account of the British Empire at its zenith.

Parker, J. *Rhodesia: Little White Island* (Pitman Publishing, 1972). The story of a white family in Rhodesia from 1955 until their departure in 1966.

Wills, A. J. *The History of Central Africa* (Oxford University Press, 1967). A comprehensive, unbiased history of Central Africa from prehistory to the middle 1960s.

Picture Credits

The author and publishers wish to thank all those who have given permission for the reproduction of copyright illustrations on the following pages: the Radio Times Hulton Picture Library, *frontispiece*, 11–12, 14–15, 20–21, 24–25, 28, 30, 32–33, 35–36, 38–40, 43–44, 46, 48, 51, 54, 56, 62, 64, 67, 69–72, 78 *top*, 81–84, 87; Mary Evans Picture Library, 18, 27, 29, 31; De Beers Consolidated Mines Ltd., 16–17, 22, 34, 74, 77, 78 *below*; All remaining illustrations belong to the Wayland Picture Library.

Index